NIKOLA TESLA MAN AHEAD OF HIS TIME

Nikola Tesla, Man Ahead of His Time (How to Build a UFO)

X FILES

(Word processor parameters LM=8, RM=75, TM=2, BM=2)

Taken from KeelyNet BBS

Sponsored by Vangard Sciences

PO BOX 1031

Mesquite, TX 75150

October 15, 1990

Listed on KeelyNet as UFO6.ZIP

Published by Axum Publications 2012

The following article was published as a two part series in the February and March issues of "The UFO Enigma", this is the Newsletter of the UFO Study Group of Greater St. Louis, Inc.

NIKOLA TESLA

MAN AHEAD OF HIS TIME

(Or How To Build a UFO)

By Bill Jones

Nikola Tesla, inventor of alternating current motors, did the basic research for constructing electromagnetic field lift-and-drive aircraft/space craft. From 1891 to 1893, he gave a set of lectures and demonstrations to groups of electrical engineers.

As part of each show, Tesla stood in the middle of the stage, using his 6' 6" height, with an assistant on either side, each 7 feet away. All 3 men wore thick cork or rubber shoe soles to avoid being electrically grounded. Each assistant held a wire, part of a high voltage, low current circuit. When Tesla raised his arms to each side, violet colored electricity jumped harmlessly across the gaps between the men. At high voltage and frequency in this arrangement, electricity flows over a

surface, even the skin, rather than into it. This is a basic circuit which could be used by aircraft / spacecraft.

The hull is best made double, of thin, machinable, slightly flexible ceramic. This becomes a good electrical insulator, has no fire danger, resists any damaging effects of severe heat and cold, and has the hardness of armor, besides being easy for magnetic fields to pass through. The inner hull is covered on its outside by wedge shaped thin metal sheets of copper or aluminum, bonded to the ceramic.

Each sheet is 3 to 4 feet wide at the horizontal rim of the hull and tapers to a few inches wide at the top of the hull for the top set of metal sheets, or at the bottom for the bottom set of sheets. Each sheet is separated on either side from the next sheet by 1 or 2 inches of uncovered ceramic hull. The top set of sheets and bottom set of sheets are separated by about 6 inches of uncovered ceramic hull around the horizontal rim of the hull.

Page 1

The outer hull protects these sheets from being short-circuited by windblown metal foil (Air Force radar confusing chaff), heavy rain or concentrations of gasoline or kerosene fumes. If Unshielded, fuel fumes could be electrostatically attracted to the hull sheets, burn and form carbon deposits across the insulating gaps between the sheets, causing a short-circuit. The space, the outer hull with a slight negative charge, would absorb hits from micro-meteorites and cosmic rays (protons moving at near the speed of light). Any danger of this type that doesn't already have a negative electric charge would get a negative charge in hitting the outer hull, and be repelled by the metal sheets before it could hit the inner hull. This wouldn't work well on a very big meteor, I might add. The hull can be made in a variety of shapes; sphere, football, disc, or streamlined rectangle or triangle, as long as these

metal sheets, "are of considerable area and arranged along ideal enveloping surfaces of very large radii of curvature," p. 85. "My Inventions", by Nikola Tesla.

The power plant for this machine can be a nuclear fission or fusion reactor for long range and long-term use to run a steam engine which turns the generators. A short range machine can use a hydrogen oxygen fuel cell to run a low-voltage motor to turn the generators, occasionally recharging by hovering next to high voltage power lines and using antennas mounted on the outer hull to take in the electricity. The short-range machine can also have electricity beamed to it from a generating plan on a long-range aircraft / spacecraft or on the ground.

(St. Louis Post-Dispatch, Nov. 24, 1987, Vol 109, No. 328, "The Forever Plane" by Geoffrey Rowan, p.D1, D7.) ("Popular Science", Vol 232, No. 1, Jan. 1988, "Secret of Perpetual Flight? Beam Power Plane," by Arthur Fisher, p. 62-65, 106)

One standard for the generators is to have the same number of magnets as field coils. Tesla's preferred design was a thin disc holding 480 magnets with 480 field coils wired in series surrounding it in close tolerance. At 50 revolutions per minute, it produces 19,400 cycles per second. The electricity is fed into a number of large capacitors, one for each metal sheet. An automatic switch, adjustable in timing by the pilot, closes, and as the electricity jumps across the switch, back and forth, it raises its own frequency; a switch being used for each capacitor.

The electricity goes into a Tesla transformer; again, one transformer for each capacitor. In an oil tank to insulate the windings and for cooling, and supported internally by wood, or plastic, pipe and fittings, each Tesla transformer looks like a short wider pipe that is moved along a longer, narrower pipe by an insulated non-electric cable handle. The short pipe, the primary, is 6 to 10 windings (loops) of wire connected in series to the long pipe. The secondary is 460 to 600 windings, at the low

voltage and frequency end. The insulated non-electric cable handle is used through a set of automatic controls to move the primary coil to various places on the secondary coil. This is the frequency control. The secondary coil has a low frequency and voltage end and a maximum voltage and frequency end. The greater the frequency the electricity, the more it pushes against the earth's electrostatic and electromagnetic fields. The electricity comes out of the transformer at the high voltage end and goes by wire through the ceramic hull to the wide end of the metal sheet. The electricity jumps out on and flows over the metal sheet, giving off a very strong electromagnetic field, controlled by the transformer. At the narrow end of the metal sheet, most of the high-voltage push having been given off, the electricity goes back by wire through the hull to a circuit breaker box (emergency shut off), then to the other side of the generators.

In bright sunlight, the aircraft / spacecraft may seem surrounded by hot air, a slight magnetic distortion of the light. In semi-darkness and

night, the metal sheets glow, even though the thin ceramic outer hull, with different colors. The visible light is a by-product of the electricity flowing over the metal sheets, according to the frequencies used.

Descending, landing or just starting to lift from the ground, the transformer primaries are near the secondary weak ends and therefore, the bottom set of sheets glow a misty red. Red may also appear at the front of the machine when it is moving forward fast, lessening resistance up front. Orange appears for slow speed. Orange-yellow are for airplane-type speeds. Green and blue are for higher speeds. With a capacitor addition, making it oversized for the circuit, the blue becomes bright white, like a searchlight, with possible risk of damaging the metal sheets involved. The highest visible frequency is violet, like Tesla's stage demonstrations, used

for the highest speed along with the bright white. The colors are nearly coherent, of a single frequency, like a laser.

A machine built with a set of super conducting magnets would simplify and reduce electricity needs from a vehicle's transformer circuits to the point of flying along efficiently and hovering with little electricity.

When Tesla was developing arc lights to run on alternating current, there was a bothersome high-pitched whine, whistle, or buzz, due to the electrodes rapidly heating and cooling. Tesla put this noise in the ultrasonic range with the special transformer already mentioned. The aircraft / spacecraft gives off such noises when working at low frequencies.

Timing is important in the operation of this machine. For every 3 metal sheets, when the middle one is briefly turned off, the sheet on either side is energized, giving off the magnetic field. The next instant, the middle sheet is energized, while the sheet on either side is briefly turned off. There is a time delay in the capacitors recharging themselves, so at any time, half of all the metal sheets are energized and the other half are recharging, alternating all around the inner hull. This balances the machine, giving it very good stability. This balance is less when fewer of the circuits are in use.

Fairly close, the aircraft / spacecraft produces heating of persons and objects on the ground; but by hovering over an area at low altitude for maybe 5 or 10 minutes, the machine also produces a column of very cold air down to the ground. As air molecules get into the strong magnetic fields that the machine is transmitting out, the air molecules become polarized and from lines, or strings, of air molecules. The normal movement of the air is stopped, and there is suddenly a lot more room for air molecules in this area, so more air pours in. This expansion and the lack of normal air motion make the area intensely cold.

This is also the reason that the aircraft / spacecraft can fly at supersonic speeds without making sonic booms. As air flows over the hull, top and bottom, the air molecules form lines as they go through the magnetic fields of the metal sheet circuits. As the air molecules are left behind, they keep their line arrangements for a short time, long enough to cancel out the sonic boom shock waves.

Outside the earth's magnetic field, another propulsion system must be used, which relies on the first. You may have read of particle accelerators, or cyclotrons, or atom smashers. A particle accelerator is a circular loop of pipe that, in cross-section, is oval. In a physics laboratory, most of the air in it is pumped out. The pipe loop is given a static electric charge, a small amount of hydrogen or other gas is given the same electric charge so the particles won't stick to the pipe. A set of electromagnets all around the pipe loop turn on and off, one after the other, pushing with one magnetic pole and pulling with the next, until those gas particles are racing around the pipe loop at nearly the speed of light. Centrifugal force makes the particles speed closer to the outside edge of the pipe loop, still within the pipe. The particles

break down into electrons, or light and other wavelengths, protons or cosmic rays, and neutrons if more than hydrogen is put in the accelerator.

At least 2 particle accelerators are used to balance each other and counter each other's tendency to make the craft spin. Otherwise, the machine would tend to want to start spinning, following the direction of the force being applied to the particles. The accelerators push in opposite directions.

As the pilot and crew travel in space, outside the magnetic field of a world, water from a tank is electrically separated into oxygen and hydrogen.

Waste carbon dioxide that isn't used for the onboard garden, and hydrogen (helium if the machine is using a fusion reactor) is slowly, constantly fed into the inside curves of both accelerators.

The high speed particles go out through straight lengths of pipe, charged like the loops and in speeding out into space, push the machine along. Doors control which pips the particles leave from. This allows very long range acceleration and later deceleration at normal (earth) gravity. This avoids the severe problems of weightlessness, including lowered physical abilities of the crew.

It is possible to use straight-line particle accelerators, even as few as one per machine, but these don't seem as able to get the best machine speed for the least amount of particles pushed out.

Page 4

Using a constant acceleration of 32.2 feet per second per second provides earth normal gravity in deep space and only gravities of stress in leaving the earth's gravity field. It takes, not counting air resistance, 18 minutes, 58.9521636 seconds to reach the 25,000 miles per hour speed to leave the earth's gravity field. It takes about 354 days, 12 hours, 53 minutes and 40 seconds (about) to reach the speed of light - 672,487,072.7 miles per hour. It takes the same distance to decelerate as it does to speed up, but this cuts down the time delay that one would have in conventional chemical rocketry enormously, for a long journey.

A set of superconducting magnets can be charged by metal sheet circuits, within limits, to whatever frequency is needed and will continue to transmit that magnetic field frequency almost indefinitely. A shortwave radio can be used to find the exact frequencies that an aircraft / spacecraft is using, for each of the colors it may show whole a color television can show the same overall color

frequency that the nearby, but not extremely close, craft is using This is limited, as a machine traveling at the speed of a jet airliner may broadcast in a frequency range usually used for radar sets.

The craft circuits override lower frequency, lower voltage electric circuits within and near their electromagnetic fields. One source briefly mentioned a 1941 incident, where a shortwave radio was used to override automobile ignition systems, up to 3 miles away. When the shortwave radio was turned off, the cars could work again. How many UFO encounters have been reported in which automobile ignition systems have suddenly stopped?

I figure that things would not be at all pleasant for drivers of modern cars with computer controlled engine and ignition systems.

Computer circuitry is sensitive to small changes in voltage and a temporary wrong-way voltage surge may wipe the computer memory out. It could mean that a number of drivers would suddenly be stranded with their cars not working should such a craft fly low over a busy highway. Only diesel engines, already warmed up, and Stanley Steamer type steam engine cares are able to continue working in a strong electromagnetic field.

In May, 1988, it was reported that the U.S. Army had lost 5 Blackhawk helicopters and 22 crewmen in crashes caused by ordinary commercial radio broadcasting overriding the computer control circuits of those helicopters. Certainly, computer circuits for for this aircraft / spacecraft can and must be designed to overcome this weakness.

One construction arrangement for this craft to avoid such interference is for the metal sheet circuits to be more sharply tuned. Quartz or other crystals can be used in capacitors; in a

very large number of low-powered, single frequency circuits, or as part of a frequency control for the metal sheet circuits.

The aircraft / spacecraft easily overrides lower frequency and lower voltage electric circuits up to a 6 mile wide circle around it, but the effect is usually not tuned for such a drastic show. It can be used for fire fighting: by hovering at a medium-low height at low frequency, it forms a double negative pole magnet of itself and the ground, the sides being a rotation of positive magnetic pole.

Page 5

It polarizes the column of air in this field. The air becomes icy cold. If it wouldn't put the fire out, it would slow it down.

NIKOLA TESLA MAN AHEAD OF HIS TIME

Tesla went broke in the early 1900's building a combination radio and electric power broadcasting station. The theory and experiments were correct but the financiers didn't want peace and prosperity for all.

The Japanese physicist who developed superconducting material with strong magnetism allows for a simplified construction of the aircraft / spacecraft. Blocks of this material can be used in place of the inner hull metal sheets. By putting electricity in each block, the pilot can control the strength of the magnetic field it gives off and can reduce the field strength by draining some of the electric charge. This allows the same amount of work to be done with vastly less electricity used to do it.

It is surprising that Jonathan Swift, in his "Gulliver's Travels", 1726, third book, "A Voyage to Laputa", described an imagined magnetic flying island that comes close to being what a large superconducting aircraft / spacecraft can be built as, using little or no electric power to hover and mover around.

TESLA INVENTIONS

NIKOLA TESLA MAN AHEAD OF HIS TIME

NIKOLA TESLA MAN AHEAD OF HIS TIME

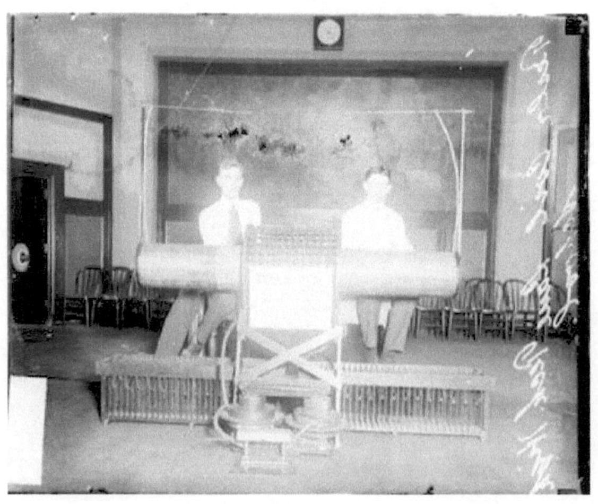

NIKOLA TESLA MAN AHEAD OF HIS TIME

7 INVENTIONS STOLEN FROM TESLA

NIKOLA TESLA MAN AHEAD OF HIS TIME

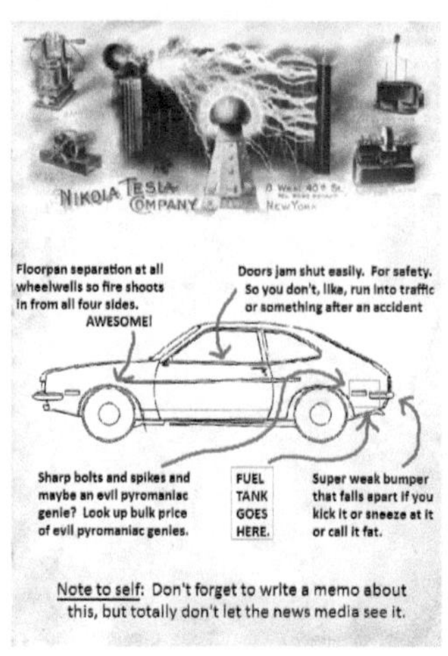

NIKOLA TESLA MAN AHEAD OF HIS TIME

NIKOLA TESLA MAN AHEAD OF HIS TIME

NIKOLA TESLA MAN AHEAD OF HIS TIME

X-RAY MACHINE

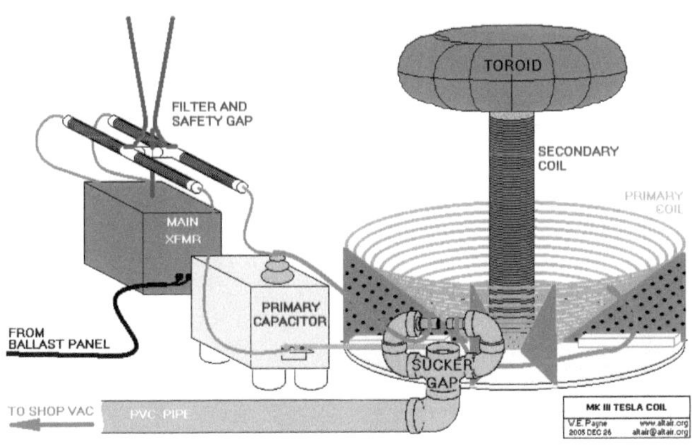

TESLA COIL

TESLA A. C. TOWER

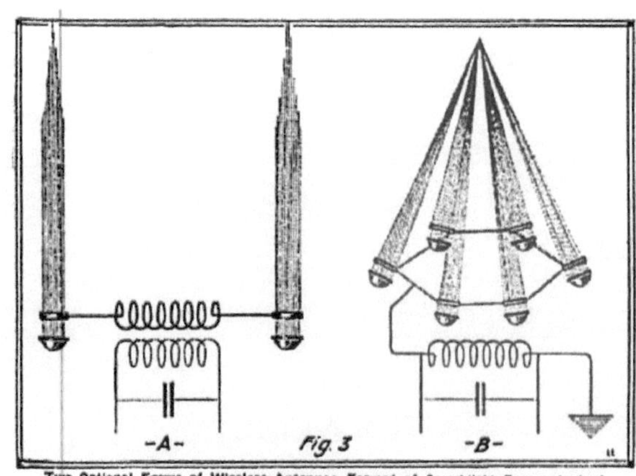

Two Optional Forms of Wireless Antennae Formed of Searchlight Beams—Ionized Atmospheric Streams.

DEATH RAY

NIKOLA TESLA MAN AHEAD OF HIS TIME

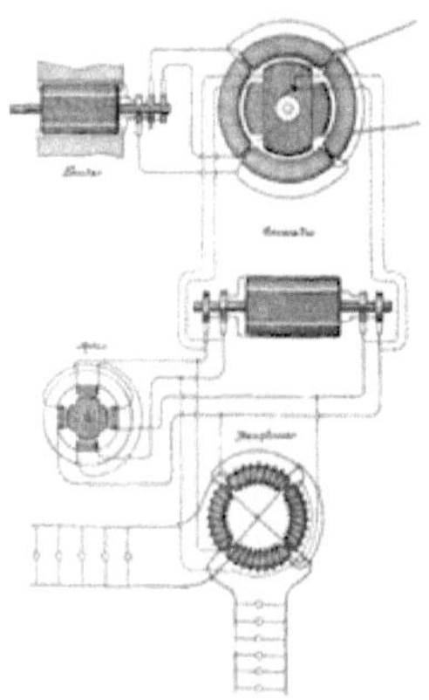

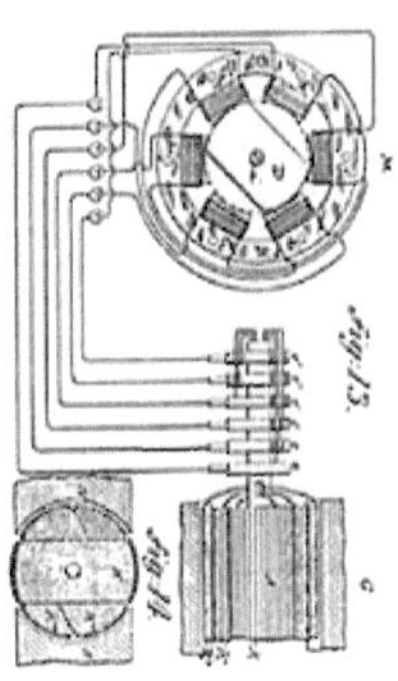

NIKOLA TESLA MAN AHEAD OF HIS TIME

TESLA WORKING ON AN INVENTION

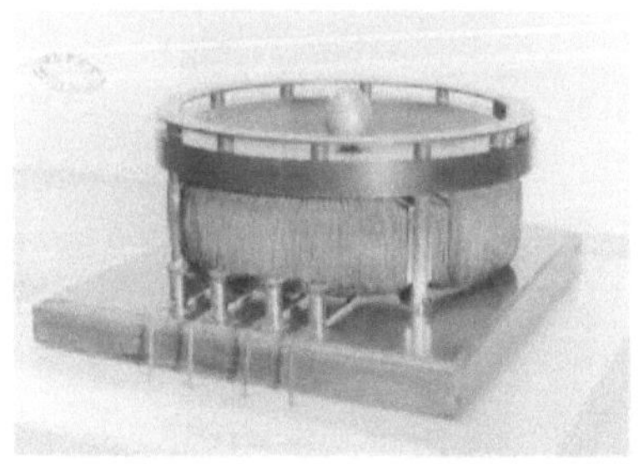

TESLA'S EGG OF COLUMBUS

NIKOLA TESLA MAN AHEAD OF HIS TIME

TESLA COIL

TESLA, INVENTOR OF THE RADIO

NIKOLA TESLA MAN AHEAD OF HIS TIME

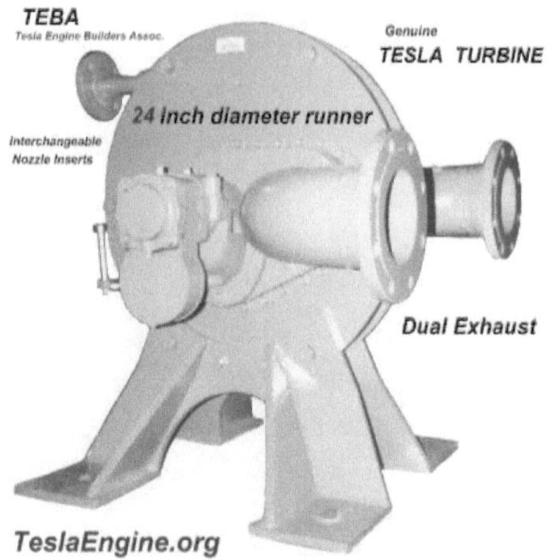

TESLA TURBINE ENGINE

A.M. INTERVIEW

There are no UFOs, just U.S. secrets

TESLA'S INVENTIONS

NIKOLA TESLA MAN AHEAD OF HIS TIME

THE BOSTON SUNDAY GLOBE—DECEMBER 18, 1904. 3

INVENTIONS OF TESLA.

A Man Whose Mind Works While He Sleeps.

"Let us suppose I have my plant at Niagara and you are running a sugar factory in Australia: by my discoveries it will be possible to send you 100 or 500 or 1000 horse power for your factory and to supply the same regularly by the force furnished from Niagara Falls."

—Nikola Tesla.

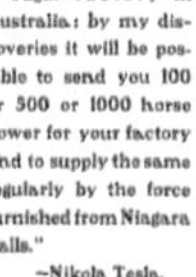

TESLA IN HIS WORKSHOP.

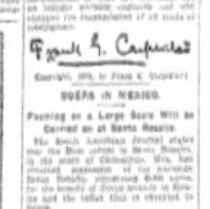

BONNEY MEMORIAL IN LOWELL.

One of the Most Artistic Monuments in New England, if Not in the United States—Erected by Hon Charles S. Lilley in Honor of His Wife and Her Parents—Ideal Statue of Heroic Size Was Bought When in the Clay.

BONNEY MEMORIAL—"THE NEW LIFE."

PUMP OUSTS A WELL SWEEP.

OLD WELL SWEEP.

LITTLE COLORED GIRL WAS THE NURSE OF BLAINE WHEN A BABY.

Aunt Keziah Jackson

NIKOLA TESLA MAN AHEAD OF HIS TIME

TESLA'S TOWER

Amazing Scheme of the Great Inventor to Draw Millions of Volts of Electricity Through the Air From Niagara Falls and Then Feed It Out to Cities, Factories and Private Houses from the Tops of the Towers WITHOUT WIRES.

NIKOLA TESLA MAN AHEAD OF HIS TIME

BOOKS BY FAHEEM JUDAH-EL D.D.

AND

AXUM PUBLICATIONS

NIKOLA TESLA MAN AHEAD OF HIS TIME

NIKOLA TESLA MAN AHEAD OF HIS TIME

THE REAL
MEANING OF SUFI
REVISED EDITION

FAHEEM JUDAH-EL

NIKOLA TESLA MAN AHEAD OF HIS TIME

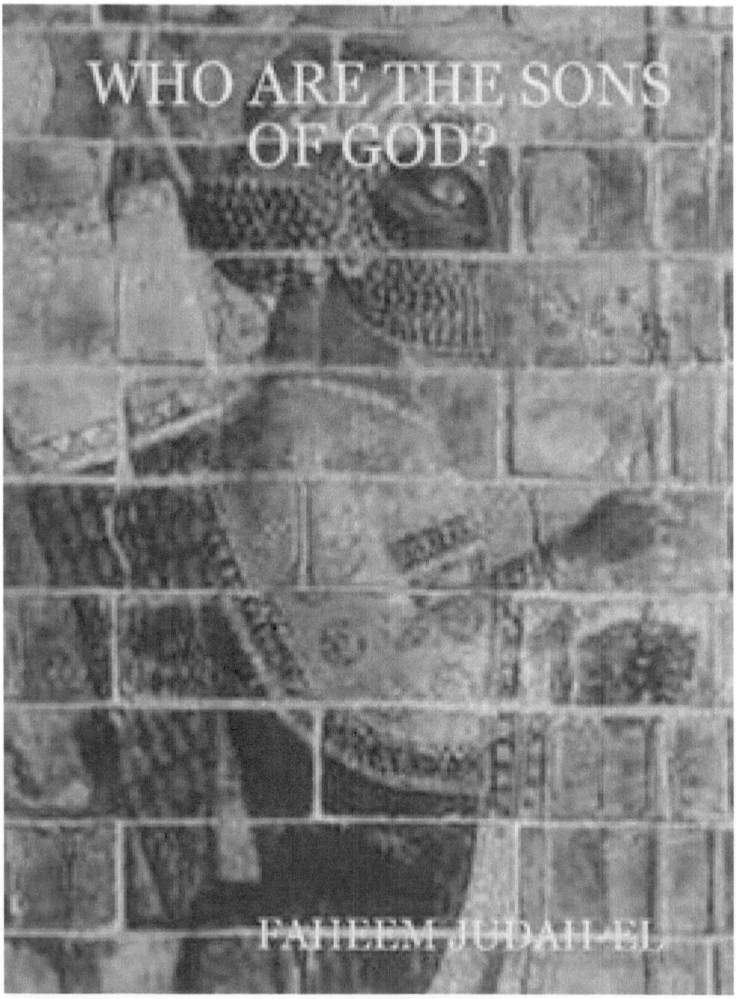

WHO ARE THE SONS OF GOD?

FAHEEM JUDAH-EL

NIKOLA TESLA MAN AHEAD OF HIS TIME

SPIRITUAL
ARCHAEOLOGY
THE FIRST
DEGREE

FAHEEM JUDAH-EL

NIKOLA TESLA MAN AHEAD OF HIS TIME

THE ORDER OF MELCHIZEDEK STUDY BOOK ONE

ALEPH

DR. FAHEEM JUDAH-EL

NIKOLA TESLA MAN AHEAD OF HIS TIME

www.lulu.com/spotlight/egipt999

NOTES

NOTES

www.ingramcontent.com/pod-product-compliance
Ingram Content Group UK Ltd.
Pitfield, Milton Keynes, MK11 3LW, UK
UKHW041905190726
13854UKWH00003B/1101